A
TREASURY
OF
GROSS
JOKES

A TREASURY OF GROSS JOKES

● ● ● ● ●

Julius Alvin

KENSINGTON BOOKS
http://www.kensingtonbooks.com

KENSINGTON BOOKS are published by
Kensington Publishing Corp.
850 Third Avenue
New York, NY 10022

ISBN 0-7582-0422-1

First Kensington Trade Paperback Printing: December, 2003
10 9 8 7 6 5 4 3 2 1

Printed in the United States of America

For Kris Gilpin,
a bigger screwball than me.

CONTENTS

NOW, THAT'S GROSS

• • • • • • •

What's the definition of gross?

When a varsity cheerleader does a split and eight class rings fall out!

• • •

What's the fourth biggest lie?

It's only a cold sore!

• • •

What's the definition of virginity?

A big issue over a little tissue!

• • •

A third-grade schoolteacher was trying to explain to her class the difference between singular and plural. She said, "What is it if one woman looks out a window?"

Little Charlotte said, "Singular."

"Very good," said the teacher. "What is it if three women are looking out of a window?"

Little Johnny mumbled just loud enough for all to hear, "A whorehouse."

• • •

What has a whole bunch of little balls and screws old ladies?

A bingo machine.

• • •

Did you hear about the flasher who considered retirement?

He decided to stick it out for another year!

• • •

What makes men chase women they have no intention of marrying?

The same urge that makes dogs chase cars they have no intention of driving!

• • •

A stockbroker calls a client and says, "I have good news and bad news."
The client says, "Tell me the bad news first."
The stockbroker says, "I lost all of your money."
Sam says, "What's the good news?"
The stockbroker says, "I got laid last night."

• • •

How can you tell if it is really, truly cold in your house?

It cures your girlfriend's headache.

• • •

A father took his children to the zoo in order to show them the monkeys. Unfortunately, it was mating time, and the attendant explained that the monkeys had gone inside their little sanctuary to play together.

"Would they come out for some peanuts?" asked the father.

"Would you?" responded the attendant.

• • •

How can you tell if you're a loser?

Your girlfriend wants to have sex in the backseat of your car and insists that you drive.

• • •

What is the difference between a blonde and a brunette?

A brunette is looking for Mr. Right. A blonde is looking for Mr. Right Now.

• • •

What does a girl with bulimia call two fingers?

Dessert.

• • •

The stock clerk inside the grocery store approached to help a man who had been going around inside the store yelling, "Crisco! Crisco!" and informed him that that particular product was against the back wall.

"No, you don't understand," the man said, "I am just looking for my wife."

"You call your wife 'Crisco'?"

"Only in public places. At home I refer to her as 'Lard-ass.'"

• • •

How do they advertise BMWs in Harlem?

"You stole the radio—now steal the car!"

• • •

Why did God create man first?

Because he didn't want a woman around telling him what to do.

• • •

What was the sequel to White Men Can't Jump?

Black Men Never Shut the Fuck Up at the Movies

• • •

Drowsing contentedly after an afternoon of making love in bed, suddenly a couple hears the sound of a car pulling up outside.

Dreamily the woman whispers, "Uh-oh, quick, get moving; that's my husband."

Quick as a flash, the man jumps out of bed, rushes to the window, and suddenly stops dead.

"What d'ya mean?" he bellows. "I AM your husband!"

• • •

How do you quit masturbating?

You go cold jerky.

• • •

What's the definition of the "perfect breakfast?"

Your son is on the box of Wheaties, your mistress is on the cover of *Playboy,* and your wife is on the back of the milk carton.

• • •

Why did the guy from Montana break up with his girlfriend?

Because the sheep wanted a commitment.

• • •

Mr. and Mrs. Fitzgerald came before the judge for their divorce hearing.

The judge asked, "What are the grounds?"

Mrs. Fitzgerald said, "Cruel and inhuman punishment. He tied me to the bed and then forced me to sing *'Macarena'* while he pissed all over me."

The judge responded, "My God, that is horrible!"

She replied, "Yes, Your Honor! He knows how much I hate that song."

• • •

Why is the space between a woman's breasts and hips called a waist?

Because there is room there for another pair of tits.

• • •

How do you know you're from Alabama?

You've been fired from your construction job because of your appearance.

• • •

How do you REALLY know you're from Alabama?

After having sex, you've asked your date to roll the window down.

• • •

A blonde teenage girl comes home from school and asks her mother, "Is it true what Rita just told me—babies come out of the same place where boys put their thingies?"

"Yes, dear," replies her mother, pleased that the subject has finally come up and she won't have to explain it to her daughter.

"But then, when I have a baby," responds the blonde teenager, "won't it knock my teeth out?"

• • •

Why must blondes always whistle while they are on the toilet?

To remind themselves which end to wipe.

• • •

What do you call a huge fart in the men's room of a bus station?

A faggot love call.

• • •

What do your boss and a Slinky have in common?

They're both fun to watch tumble down the stairs.

• • •

Tex goes into a British restaurant with his wife. The waiter approaches the table and asks for their order.

"I'll have your biggest, juiciest London broil," he says.

"But, sir, what about the mad cow?" asks the waiter.

"Oh," answers Tex, "she'll order for herself."

• • •

Who's the poorest guy in West Virginia?

The Tooth Fairy.

• • •

Why did the basketball player marry the midget?

He was nuts over her.

• • •

Melvin's wife asks, "Honey, do these jeans make my ass look like the side of the house?"
He says, "No, our house isn't blue."

• • •

Chatting with her next-door neighbor, Amy said, "I feel really good today. I started the day with an act of unselfish generosity. I gave a five-dollar bill to a bum."

"You gave a bum five dollars? That's a lot of money to be handing out like that. What did your husband say?" her neighbor asked.

"He said, 'Thanks!'"

• • •

How can you tell a woman is really ugly?

A cannibal takes one look at her and orders a salad.

• • •

Why do women fake orgasms?

They think we give a shit.

• • •

A dating Amish couple, Elizabeth and Eli, are riding down the road in their buggy. It's mid-January and very cold. Elizabeth says to Eli, "My feet are frozen solid."

Eli says, "Well, put them in my lap. I'll rub them and warm them up."

Elizabeth does so, and after a while she asks, "Eli, what's that hard thing in your pants?"

Eli answers, "That's my penis; it's frozen solid. Maybe you can rub it and warm it up?"

The next morning Elizabeth comes down for breakfast and asks her mother, "Ma, what do you know about penises?"

Her mother asks, "I don't know, what do YOU know about penises?"

Elizabeth replies, "Well, they sure are messy when they melt!"

• • •

What's the definition of a surprise?

A fart with a lump in it.

• • •

What's the definition of pocket pool?

What a mother kangaroo has until her children are toilet trained.

• • •

How did the teenager know he had really bad acne?

His dog called him "Spot."

• • •

A noted sex therapist realized that people often lie about the frequency of their encounters, so he devised a test to tell for certain how often someone had sex. To prove his theory, he filled up an auditorium with people and went down the line asking each person to smile. Using the size of the person's smile, the therapist was able to guess accurately how often each person had sex. The last man in line was grinning from ear to ear.

"Twice a day," the therapist guessed, but was surprised when the man said no. "Once a day, then?" said the therapist. Again the answer was no. "Twice a week?" "No." "Twice a month?" "No."

When the doctor asked, "Once a year?" the man finally said yes.

The therapist was angry that his theory hadn't worked with this individual, and he asked the man, "Then what the heck are you so happy about?"

The man answered, "Tonight's the night!"

• • •

How can you tell if a guy is a real loser?

His only sex life is when his doctor tells him to cough.

• • •

How do women keep a man happy in bed?

They move the TV into the bedroom.

• • •

Why do men choose showers over baths?

That's the only way they can piss while getting clean.

• • •

A woman and a man are involved in a car accident; it's a bad one. Both of their cars are totally demolished, but amazingly, neither of them is hurt. After they crawl out of their cars, the woman says, "So you're a man; that's interesting. I'm a woman. Wow, just look at our cars! There's nothing left, but fortunately we are unhurt. This must be a sign from God that we should meet and be friends and live together in peace for the rest of our days."

The man replied, "I agree with you completely. This must be a sign from God!"

The woman continued, "And look at this; here's another miracle. My car is completely demolished, but the bottle of wine that was in my trunk didn't break. Surely God wants us to drink this wine and celebrate our good fortune." Then she hands the bottle to the man.

The man nods his head in agreement, opens it and drinks half the bottle, and then hands it back to the woman. She hands it back to the man.

The man asks, "Aren't you having any?"

The woman replies, "No. I think I'll just wait for the police."

• • •

How do you get five hundred cows into a barn?

Hang up a Bingo sign.

• • •

Did you hear about the guy who got his vasectomy at Sears?

Every time he gets a hard-on, his garage door opens.

• • •

Why do women have smaller feet than men?

So that they can stand closer to the sink.

• • •

A man was sitting at a bar, morosely staring at his untouched beer. The bartender walked over and asked, "What's the problem, pal?"

"My brother just told me there's a sperm bank in his neighborhood that pays forty dollars for a donation."

"Yeah, so?"

"Don't you realize?" the man cried. "I've let a fortune slip through my fingers!"

• • •

The Reverend John Fuzz was pastor of a small congregation in a little town. One day he was walking down Main Street and he happened to notice a female member of his congregation sitting in the town bar, drinking beer. The preacher thought this was sinful and not something a member of his congregation should do, so he walked through the open door of the bar and sat down next to the woman.

"Mrs. Fitzgerald," he said sternly, "this is no place for a member of my congregation. Why don't you let me take you home?"

"Shhhure," she said, obviously very drunk.

When Mrs. Fitzgerald stood up from the bar, she began to weave back and forth. The preacher realized that she had had too much to drink, and he grabbed hold of her arms to steady her. When he did, they both lost their balance and tumbled to the floor. After rolling around for a few seconds, the preacher wound up lying on top of Mrs. Fitzgerald, her skirt hiked up to her waist.

The bartender looked over the bar and said, "Hey, buddy, we won't have any of that carrying on in this bar."

The preacher looked up at the bartender and said, "But you don't understand, I'm Pastor Fuzz!"

The bartender said, "Well, heck, if you're that far along, you might as well finish the job."

• • •

Pete and Dud have been seriously drinking and, on the way home from the pub, have to go for a pee in the bushes. While they are relieving themselves, Pete says, "I wish I had a dick like my friend Winston, that I could hold with four fingers."

Dud says, "But you are holding it with four fingers."

Pete says, "Yeah, but I'm pissing on three of them."

• • •

A man who has been undecided about his sexuality all his life finally decides he is going to try sex with another man. He goes to the local gay bar and orders a drink.

The bartender says, "You look nervous—first time?"

"Yes," says the man.

"Not to worry," the bartender says. "I'll take you back to my house and have sex with you. If you don't like it, make the noise of an animal, and if you do like it, just sing a song." The man agrees and goes home with the barman at the end of his shift. They go into his bedroom, and the bartender strips him and starts riding his ass. He hears his new friend screaming, "Moooooo, moooooo, *Moooon River . . .*"

• • •

What's the difference between a boyfriend and a husband?

Forty-five minutes.

• • •

How can you tell if your husband's dead?

The sex is the same, but you get the remote.

• • •

How many men does it take to change a lightbulb?

None, they just sit there in the dark and complain.

• • •

What do men and floor tiles have in common?

If you lay them properly the first time, you can walk all over them for life.

• • •

Why do men want to marry virgins?

They can't stand criticism.

• • •

What's a man's view of safe sex?

A padded headboard.

• • •

Do you know why women fake orgasms?

Because men fake foreplay.

• • •

What do you call a smart blonde?

A golden retriever.

• • •

Who is the most popular guy at the nudist colony?

The guy who can carry a cup of coffee in each hand and a dozen donuts.

• • •

Who is the most popular girl in the nudist colony?

The one who can eat the last donut.

• • •

What's the difference between a battery and a man?

A battery has a positive side.

• • •

What's the difference between a tribe of pygmies and women's track team?

One is a group of cunning runts.

· · ·

There once was a woman who went to the doctor. When the doctor saw her, he asked her what was wrong. She replied, "I ache all over."

So the doctor began to check her out. First he checked out her breasts, and she asked him if that was the problem. He replied, "Nope, nothing wrong with them."

Then he checked her thighs out and told her there's nothing wrong with them. By this time, he was so horny he couldn't stand it any longer, and he began to fuck her hard. After he finished, she asked him if there was anything wrong, and he replied, "No."

She said, "Oh, good. Now we both have the clap, and I feel much better."

· · ·

What do a thousand battered women have in common?

They never shut the fuck up.

• • •

How are women and tornadoes alike?

They both moan when they come and take the house when they leave.

• • •

How many male chauvinists does it take to open a beer can?

None, because the bitch better have it open when she hands it to you.

• • •

How do you give a woman an orgasm?

Who cares?

• • •

How many women does it take to change a light-bulb?

Two. One to screw it in and one to suck my dick.

• • •

What do you say to a feminist with no arms and no legs?

Nice tits, bitch.

• • •

What's the hardest part about a sex-change operation?

Removing half the brain.

• • •

What's the definition of a woman?

Life support for a vagina.

• • •

27

What do women and condoms have in common?

Both spend more time in your wallet than on your dick.

• • •

Why can't Helen Keller drive?

She's a woman.

• • •

What is the definition of making love?

Something a woman does while a guy is fucking her.

• • •

How do we know God is a man?

If God were a woman, sperm would taste like chocolate.

• • •

What's the most intelligent thing to come out of a woman's mouth?

Einstein's dick.

• • •

Why don't women fart?

Their mouths are never shut long enough to build up any pressure.

• • •

What's the best thing about receiving oral sex from a woman?

The ten minutes of silence.

• • •

What do you tell a woman with two black eyes?

Nothing, you've already told her twice.

• • •

What does a woman do after she gets out of the battered women's shelter?

The dishes, if she knows what's good for her.

• • •

Why did God give women pussies?

So men would talk to them.

• • •

Why can't women ski?

Because there's no snow between the kitchen and the bedroom.

• • •

Why do men bring flowers to their women in the hospital?

Because a bale of hay is too heavy.

• • •

Why do women get periods?

Because they deserve them.

• • •

Why don't women wear watches?

Because the microwave has a clock on it.

• • •

An intelligent man, an intelligent woman, and Santa Claus are walking down the street when they spot a fifty-dollar bill. Who picks it up?
The intelligent man. The other two don't exist.

• • •

What is wife *short for?*

Washing. Ironing, Fucking. Etc.

• • •

What's the best thing God ever did?

He invented pussy.

What's the worst thing He ever did?

He put women in charge of it.

• • •

Hear about the new route on Alaska Airlines?

It goes from JFK to JFK Junior.

• • •

Did you hear they came out with Viagra Light?

You don't get hard enough to fuck, but you look good in a bathing suit.

• • •

Why didn't the blonde pay for the new windows in her house?

The salesman said that in twelve months they'd pay for themselves.

• • •

TEN REASONS WHY IT'S GREAT TO BE A GUY

1. Phone conversations are over in thirty seconds.
2. Someday you'll be a dirty old man.
3. *Monday Night Football.*
4. Bathroom lines are 80 percent shorter.
5. All your orgasms are real.
6. Your last name stays put.
7. Nobody secretly wonders if you swallow.
8. Sex means never having to worry about your reputation.
9. You can write your name in the snow.
10. If you retain water, it's in a canteen.

• • •

TEN REASONS WHY IT SUCKS TO BE A GUY

1. If you put a woman on a pedestal and try to protect her from the rat race, you're a male chauvinist.
2. If you work too hard, there's never enough time for her.
   If you don't work hard enough, you're a good-for-nothing bum.
3. If she has a boring, repetitive job with low pay, this is exploitation.

If you have a boring, repetitive job with low pay, you should get off your ass and get something better.

4. If you get a promotion ahead of her, that's favoritism.

   If she gets a promotion ahead of you, it's equal opportunity.

5. If you mention how nice she looks, it's sexual harassment.

   If you keep quiet, it's male indifference.

6. If you cry, you're a wimp.

   If you don't, you're an insensitive bastard.

7. If you thump her, it's wife-beating.

   If she thumps you, it's self-defense.

8. If you make a decision without consulting her, you're a chauvinist.

   If she makes a decision without consulting you, she's a liberated woman.

9. If you ask her to do something she doesn't enjoy, that's domination.

   If she asks you, it's a favor.

10. If you appreciate the female form and frilly underwear, you're a pervert.

    If you don't, you're gay.

• • •

Why are women like rocks?

You skip the flat ones.

• • •

Why do women have arms?

Do you have any idea how long it would take to lick the toilet clean?

• • •

What's the difference between a pussy and a cunt?

A pussy is soft, warm, and inviting; a cunt is the person who owns it.

• • •

FIVE SIMPLE RULES WOMEN
DON'T UNDERSTAND

1. Nothing says "I love you" like a blow job in the morning.
2. Learn to work the toilet seat: if it's up, put it down.
3. If you think you're fat, you probably are. Don't ask us.
4. Don't cut your hair. Ever.
5. Don't make us guess.

• • •

How do you know the Polack has been sending E-mail?

There are a bunch of envelopes stuffed in the disk drive.

• • •

Have you heard about the new, supersensitive condoms?

After you fuck, it'll stay and talk to her.

• • •

Did you hear they've improved Viagra?

It's so strong now that you can get a hard-on with your wife.

• • •

Why did Helen Keller have wax on her fingers?

Because she was whispering sweet nothings in her boyfriend's ear.

• • •

A man is fucking his wife. He says, "Did I hurt you?"

She says, "No, why do you ask?"

He says, "You moved."

• • •

The judge says, "Please tell me why you are seeking a divorce."

The husband says, "Because I live in a two-story house."

The judge says, "What kind of reason is that? What's the matter with a two-story house?"

The husband says, "I'll tell you what's the matter. One story is, 'I have a headache,' and the other story is, 'It's that time of the month.'"

• • •

How can you tell a lady midget is having her period?

She keeps tripping on the string.

• • •

What's the biggest advantage of Alzheimer's disease?

You can cheat on your wife *with* your wife.

• • •

What does every feminist in the world need?

A good man to smack some sense into her.

• • •

What do a walrus and Tupperware have in common?

Both like a tight seal.

• • •

One afternoon a little girl excitedly approached her mother and announced that she had learned where babies come from.

Amused, the mother replied, "Really, sweetie? Why don't you tell me about it?"

The little girl explained, "Well, the mommy and daddy take off all of their clothes, and the daddy's thing sort of stands up, and the mommy puts it in her mouth, and then it sort of explodes, and that's where babies come from."

Her mom shook her head and said in a confidential tone, "Oh, honey, that's sweet, but that's not where babies come from. That's where jewelry comes from."

• • •

How can you tell when an auto mechanic just had sex?

One of his fingers is clean.

• • •

What do you call a man with a sex-change operation?

A trans-sister.

• • •

Why can't women read maps?

Because only the male mind can grasp the concept that one inch equals a mile.

• • •

When a blonde went to the dentist for the first time in years, she was prepared for bad news. Nevertheless, she was a little put out when, after some time, the dentist gasped, "Jesus, what happened to your teeth? They're all gone, and your gums are in terrible shape!"

"If it's such a big problem," retorted the blonde, "then get your face out of my lap!"

• • •

What's brown and sings rap music?

Puff Doody.

• • •

What was the last thing JFK Jr. ever said?

"You know, Carolyn, your sister's a better lay than you are."

• • •

<u>You might be from Arkansas if . . .</u>

You've ever gotten an official letter of recognition from a tobacco or beer company.

You vacuum the sheets rather than washing them.

You go to stock car races and don't need a program.

You played the banjo in your high school band.

The velvet paintings in your house were bought from an art dealer on the side of the highway.

You can't visit relatives without getting mud on your tires.

You have a Hefty bag for a passenger side window.

Your watchband is wider than any book you've ever read.

You've ever barbecued Spam on the grill.

Your new job promotion means the company foots the bill to have your name sewn on your shirts.

Your primary income involves pigs or manure.

• • •

41

What do you call a blonde with pigtails?

A blow job with handlebars.

• • •

What did the dick say to the condom?

"Cover me; I'm going in!"

• • •

Harry dies and goes to hell.

The Devil says, "You will spend eternity here, but you get to choose how you will spend it. You may choose one of these three ways." The Devil opens door number one, and Harry sees people standing on their heads on a concrete floor.

Harry says, "No way; let's move on."

The Devil opens door number two, and Harry sees people standing on their heads on a wooden floor.

Harry says, "No way; let's move on."

The Devil opens door number three, and Harry sees a bunch of people standing knee-deep in shit, drinking coffee.

Harry says, "I guess I'll take door number three."

The Devil says, "Okay, wait right here, and I'll get you a cup of coffee."

A few minutes later, Harry is drinking his coffee and says to himself, "This ain't so bad. . . ."

Then a voice comes over a loudspeaker saying, "Okay, coffee break's over; everybody back on your heads."

• • •

Why do they call a pap smear a pap smear?

Because if they called it a cunt scrape, no woman would have one.

• • •

A guy is walking past a bus stop and says to a woman, "Can I smell your cunt?"

"Fuck off; you can't smell my cunt!"

"Oh," he replies, looking slightly confused, "it must be your feet."

• • •

43

Why is my penis larger than yours?

Because I'm jerking off right now.

• • •

What's warm, bloody, and crawls up your leg?

A homesick abortion.

• • •

Three pregnant women are sitting, chatting, and knitting for their expected kids.

The first one says, "I hope that I have a baby boy, because I'm knitting a blue jumper."

The second says, "Well, I hope I have a baby girl, because I'm knitting a pink jumper."

The third woman says, "I hope my kid's a spastic, because I fucked up the sleeves on the jumper."

• • •

How do you stop a dog from humping your leg?

Pick him up and suck his dick.

• • •

What did the rabbi do with all the foreskins he snipped?

Sold them to gay guys as chewing gum.

• • •

In the beginning, God created Earth and rested. Then God created man and rested. Then God created woman. Since then, neither God nor man has rested.

• • •

My wife and I are inseparable. In fact, last week it took four state troopers and a dog.

• • •

Why do men die before their wives?

They want to.

• • •

What is the difference between a dog and a fox?

About five drinks.

• • •

A beggar walked up to a well-dressed woman shopping on Rodeo Drive and said, "I haven't eaten anything in four days."

She looked at him and said, "Man, I wish I had your willpower."

• • •

Do you know the punishment for bigamy?

Two mothers-in-law.

• • •

A boy comes home from school and asks his father, "Is it true, Dad, that in some parts of Africa a man doesn't know his wife until he marries her?"

His father replies, "That happens in every country, son."

• • •

A man placed an ad in the classifieds: *Wife wanted.* Next day he received a hundred letters. They all said the same thing: *You can have mine.*

• • •

What happens when you cross a pig with a lawyer?

Nothing. There are some things a pig won't do.

• • •

What's the difference between a lawyer and a liar?

The pronunciation.

• • •

What's the difference between a lawyer and an onion?

You cry when you cut up an onion.

• • •

What's the difference between a lawyer and a vulture?

The lawyer gets frequent flyer miles.

• • •

Why did God create snakes just before lawyers?

To practice.

• • •

What's worse than jock itch?

Four blondes at a four-way stop.

• • •

A man entered a restaurant and sat at the only open table. As he sat down, he knocked the spoon off the table with his elbow.

A nearby waiter reached into his shirt pocket, pulled out a clean spoon, and set it on the table. The diner was impressed. "Do all the waiters carry spoons in their pockets?"

The waiter replied, "Yes. Ever since we had that efficiency expert out, he determined that 17.8 percent of our diners knock the spoon off the table. By carrying clean spoons with us, we save trips to the kitchen."

The diner ate his meal. As he was paying the waiter, he commented, "Forgive the intrusion, but do you know that you have a string hanging from your fly?"

The waiter replied, "Yes, we all do. Seems that the same efficiency expert determined that we spend too much time washing our hands after using the men's room. So the other end of that string is tied to my penis. When I need to go, I simply pull the string to get my penis out, go, and return to work. Since I don't actually touch myself, there's no need to wash my hands. Saves a lot of time."

"Wait a minute," said the diner. "How do you get your penis back in your pants?"

"Well, I don't know about the other guys, but I use the spoon."

• • •

An old man goes to the doctor for a checkup. The doctor tells him, "Sir, I have some bad news. I found two problems. First, you have cancer. Second, you have Alzheimer's disease."

The old man replies, "Well, at least I don't have cancer!"

• • •

A man and his new bride took great pride in never having had illicit sex with each other prior to their wedding. In fact, they had never even seen each other naked until that day.

As the woman was getting undressed, the man stood and watched, enjoying the sight for the first time. As the woman stood naked in her glory, she told him that it was now his turn. Slowly he removed his tie and shirt. Then he took off his trousers and socks. Finally, he lowered his boxers.

The woman, staring in shock, could not believe how tiny he was. "Just whom are you supposed to please with that little thing?" she cried.

The man smiled and proudly replied, "Me!"

• • •

REALLY, REALLY GROSS

• • • • • • •

How does a man make love to a really ugly woman?

He jerks off in his hand, then throws it at her!

• • •

Why do men have orgasms?

How else would we know when to stop?

• • •

Moms have Mother's Day and dads have Father's Day. What do single guys have?

Palm Sunday.

• • •

A psychiatrist was conducting a group therapy session with four young mothers and their small children. "You all have obsessions," he observed.

To the first mother, he said, "You are obsessed with eating. You've even named your daughter Candy."

He turned to the second mom. "Your obsession is money. Again, it manifests itself in your child's name, Penny."

He turned to the third mom. "Your obsession is alcohol. Again, it manifests itself in your child's name, Brandy."

At this point the fourth mother got up, took her little boy by the hand, and whispered, "Come on, Dick, let's go."

• • •

What's the best thing to come out of a dick?

The wrinkles!

• • •

What do you get when you cross ten lesbians and ten politicians?

Twenty people who don't do dick!

• • •

What's the difference between a bitch and a whore?

A whore sleeps with everybody at the party, and a bitch sleeps with everybody at the party except you!

• • •

The redneck goes to the doctor because he's constipated. The doctor prescribes a powerful laxative and tells the redneck to come back in three days for another checkup. When the redneck comes back, the doctor asks him, "Have you moved yet?"

The redneck says he hasn't, so the doctor writes him out a prescription for a laxative that's twice as strong as the first. "Better come back in two days," the doctor tells him.

Two days later, the redneck comes back. The doctor asks, "Have you moved yet?"

The redneck says he still hasn't, so the doctor gives him a prescription for a laxative three times as strong as the first two.

Two days later, the redneck comes back, and this time he's smiling. "Can I safely assume that you've moved?" the doctor asks him.

The redneck says, "Yup, I had to. My double-wide was full of shit!"

• • •

What do you call two lesbians in a rowboat?

Fur traders!

• • •

How many homosexuals does it take to screw in a lightbulb?

One—as long as there's plenty of KY and he's really careful!

• • •

What's the difference between love, true love, and showing off?

Spitting, swallowing, and gargling!

• • •

A drunk in a bar hurls all over his own shirt. "Damn!" he says. "I hurled on my shirt again. If my wife finds out, she's gonna kill me."

"Not to worry," says the bartender as he sticks a twenty-dollar bill in the drunk's pocket. "Just tell her someone hurled on you and gave you some cash to cover the cleaning bill."

So the drunk staggers home and tells his wife

about the guy who hurled on him and about the twenty bucks. She reaches into his pocket and finds two twenties. "Why are there TWO twenties?" she asks.

The drunk replies, "Oh, yeah . . . he crapped in my pants, too."

• • •

The words most hated by men during sex: "Is it in yet?"

Three words women hate hearing during sex: "Honey, I'm home!"

• • •

What is the numeric difference between a hooker and a sperm bank?

On the average day, the hooker gets more deposits.

• • •

A brunette, a blonde, and a redhead are all in third grade. Who has the biggest boobs?

The blonde, because she's eighteen.

• • •

57

A guy walked up to a hot babe sitting at a bar and said, "What's your name?"

"Carmen."

"Hey, baby, nice name! Who named you, your mother?"

"No. I named myself," she answers.

"How did you happen to pick 'Carmen'?"

"Because I like cars and I like men," she says. "So, what's your name?"

"Beerfuck."

• • •

Hear about the mortician who was also a necrophiliac?

He just loved to bury himself in his work.

• • •

What do you do when you see six white guys beating up a black guy?

Laugh.

What do you do when you see ten white guys beating up a black guy?

You yell, "He raped my sister!"

• • •

Two drunks are sitting in a bar when one smells something foul. He turns to the other and says, "Hey, man, did you shit yourself?"

"Yeah," says the second drunk.

"Well, get out of here! Why don't you go clean yourself up?"

The second drunk says, "Because I ain't through yet."

• • •

How did the butcher get behind in his work?

He backed into the meat grinder.

• • •

What's better than playing the piano by ear?

Fiddling with your dick.

• • •

What do you call six lesbians in a hot tub?

A clambake.

• • •

Harry answers the telephone, and it's an emergency room doctor. The doctor says, "Your wife was in a serious car accident, and I have bad news and good news. The bad news is, she has lost all use of both arms and both legs and will need help eating and going to the bathroom for the rest of her life."

Harry says, "My God! What's the good news?"

The doctor says, "I'm kidding. She's dead."

• • •

How did the blonde die from drinking milk?

She was sucking so hard that the cow fell on her.

• • •

What's female Viagra?

Jewelry.

• • •

An old timer at a rest home says to another patient, "Have you got a steady girl?

The other guy says, "No, she has Parkinson's."

• • •

What is the most sensitive part of the body during masturbation?

Your ears—to listen for footsteps.

• • •

What is the definition of a tough competitor?

In a masturbation contest, he finishes first, third, and ninth.

• • •

What's the difference between pink and purple?

Your grip!

• • •

A wife greeted her husband at three in the morning, as he arrived home very drunk. She said, "You've been cheating on me, you stupid son of a bitch!"

"No, I haven't," he replied. "Honest."

"Oh, then how do you explain the lipstick on your shirt?" she asked.

"That's easy," he says. "It got there when I was wiping off my dick."

• • •

What's the difference between hard and light?

You can get to sleep with a light on.

• • •

Why is masturbation better than sex?

Because you can see what you are doing!

• • •

What do you do after you eat a vegetable?

You put her back in the wheelchair!

• • •

Harry is on his death bed, and he says to his wife, "Can you give me one last wish?"
    She says, "Anything you want."
    He says, "After I die, will you marry Charlie?"
    She says, "But I thought you hated Charlie."
    With his last breath, he says, "I do."

• • •

How do you know when there's Viagra in your chocolate bars?

After you eat it, she says, "Oh, Oh Henry!"

• • •

Why is Viagra like Disneyland?

It's a one-hour wait for a two-minute ride.

• • •

Did you hear about the first death from an overdose of Viagra?

A man took twelve pills, and his wife died.

• • •

Two drunks are standing at a whorehouse door. The first drunk says, "I heard half these broads have the clap, and that none of 'em would think twice about stealing every penny we've got."

The second drunk says, "Not so loud, or they won't let us in."

• • •

A woman walks into a shop that sells very expensive Persian rugs. She looks around and spots the perfect rug and walks over to inspect it. As she bends to feel the texture of the rug, she farts loudly. Very embarrassed, she looks around nervously to see if anyone has noticed her little accident, and hopes a salesperson does not pop up right now.

As she turns back, there, standing next to her, is a salesman. "Good day, ma'am. How may we help you today?"

She asks, "How much does this rug cost?"

He answers, "Lady, if you farted just touching it, you're gonna shit your pants when you hear what the price is."

• • •

An old guy gets a hard-on for the first time in years. He runs into the living room and says to his wife, "I forget what I'm supposed to do with this."

She says, "Why don't you wash it while you got the wrinkles out?"

• • •

Where does a redneck go for take-out food?

Highway 101.

• • •

What was the closing of the love letters the necrophiliac always mailed?

"Eventually yours."

• • •

What is a good clue that a hospital patient has AIDS?

When you see them administering his shots with a dart gun.

• • •

A trucker goes into a whorehouse and hands the madam five hundred dollars. He says, "I want your ugliest woman and a bologna sandwich."

The madam says, "For that kind of money, you could have one of my finest girls and surf and turf."

The trucker says, "I ain't horny; I'm homesick."

• • •

An old man and his wife have gone to bed. After lying in bed for a few minutes, the old man cuts a fart and says, "Seven points."

His wife rolls over and says, "What in the world was that?"

"Touchdown. I'm ahead seven to nothing."

A few minutes later the wife lets one go and says, "Touchdown, tie score."

After about ten minutes the old man farts again and says, "Touchdown! I'm ahead fourteen to seven."

Now starting to get into it, the wife quickly farts again and says, "Touchdown, tie score."

The old man, not to be outdone, strains really hard but to no avail. He can't fart! So, not to be outdone by his wife, he gives it everything he has, trying for one more fart. Straining really hard, the old man shits the bed.

The wife asks, "What in the hell was that?"

The old man replies, "Half-time . . . switch sides."

• • •

A guy is interviewing a blonde for a job. He says, "If you could have a conversation with someone, living or dead, who would it be?"

She says, "The living one."

• • •

Why shouldn't we make fun of handicapped people?

Because if it weren't for them, we wouldn't be able to find such neat parking places.

• • •

What does it mean when an Arkansas wife drools out of both sides of her mouth?

The trailer is level.

• • •

How can you tell when your girlfriend is too flat?

When she applied for a job as a topless waitress, she got hired instead as a busboy.

• • •

A guy goes up to a girl in a bar and says, "You want to play 'magic'?"
   She says, "What's that?"
   He says, "We go to my house and fuck, and then you disappear."

• • •

67

A young woman was walking through a field gathering spring flowers; she wore a sundress but no underwear. When her husband came home for lunch, she said she thought a bee might have gotten trapped up her twat. Her husband took her to the emergency room.

The doctor said to the husband, "Let's rub some honey on your penis, and maybe it will coax the bee out."

The husband said, "Hey, I'm no doctor! I brought her here for professional help."

So the doctor rubbed honey on his penis and inserted it into the woman. The husband, next to her the entire time, noticed that after a while his wife was starting to moan and sweat. He said, "Doctor, is it working?"

The doctor, thrusting away, replied, "Coaxing it out didn't work. So now I'm going to try to shoot it out."

• • •

A woman goes into a bar and orders a bottle of champagne. She takes the first glass and pours the champagne down the back of her skirt. The bartender looks amazed as she pours another glass and again tips it down her skirt back.

Finally, the bartender asks, "Why are you pouring your drinks down your skirt?"

"Well," the woman replies, "I've just won the lottery, and this is the only asshole I'm sharing it with."

• • •

Did you hear that Viagra is going to be available in liquid form?
It's called Mydixadud.

• • •

Why do sumo wrestlers shave their legs?

They don't want to be mistaken for lesbians.

• • •

What's better than winning a gold medal at the Special Olympics?

Not being a retard.

• • •

A woman goes into a hardware store and asks the clerk, "Do you have any batteries?"

"Yes," the clerk says, gesturing with his finger. "Can you come this way?"

"If I could come that way," the woman answered, "I wouldn't need the batteries."

• • •

A guy went to a travel agent and tried to book a two-week cruise for himself and his girlfriend. The travel agent said that all the ships were booked up and things were very tight, but that he would see what he could do.

A couple of days later, the travel agent phoned and said he could now get them onto a three-day cruise. The guy agreed and went to the drugstore to buy three Dramamines and three condoms.

Next day, the agent called back and said that he now could book a five-day cruise. The guy said, "I'll take it," and returned to the same pharmacy to buy two more Dramamines and two more condoms.

The following day, the travel agent called yet again and said he could now book an eight-day cruise. The guy agreed and went back to the drugstore. He asked for three more Dramamines and three more condoms.

The pharmacist looked sympathetically at him and said, "Look, if it makes you so sick, why do you keep doing it?"

• • •

Annie was talking about her sex life with her friend Joan. "My last boyfriend said he fantasized about having two girls at once."

Joan said, "Yeah, most men do. What did you tell him?"

Annie replied, "I said, 'If you can't satisfy one woman, why would you want to piss off another one?'"

• • •

How can you tell if you are in a gay amusement park?

They hand out gerbils at the tunnel of love.

• • •

Why do women have foreheads?

So you have somewhere "else" to kiss them after you come in their mouths.

• • •

What is a blonde who stands on her head?

A brunette who smells bad.

• • •

The doctor approached the husband who was in the waiting room while his wife was being examined. The doctor said, "I have good news and bad news.

"What's the bad news?"

"Your wife has syphilis."

The husband exclaimed, "What could possibly be 'good news' with a situation like that?"

The doctor replied, "She didn't get it from you."

• • •

What's the definition of a shit-head?

A brown-noser with no brakes.

• • •

What is the best way to get even with your wife?

Dip her vibrator in Tabasco sauce.

• • •

What is the definition of bad luck?

Reaching for your penis enlarger in the dark and grabbing the blender instead.

• • •

Little Johnny walks in on his parents while they are in the act of making love. He says, "Hey, Dad! What are you doing?"

His father says, "I'm filling your mother's tank."

Johnny says, "Oh, yeah? Well, you should get a model that gets better mileage. The milkman filled her this morning."

• • •

What do a nearsighted gynecologist and a puppy have in common?

A wet nose.

• • •

How is a pussy like a warm toilet seat?

They both feel good, but you can't help wondering who was there before you.

• • •

What is the difference between dating and marriage?

When you're dating, she's hard to get; during marriage, she's impossible to get.

• • •

A guy calls his wife from the emergency room. He tells her that his finger got cut off at the construction site where he was working.

"Oh, my God!!" cries the woman. "The whole finger?"

"No," replies the guy. "The one next to it!"

• • •

What do you call an Amish guy with his hand up a horse's ass?

A mechanic.

• • •

Three old men were talking about the best thing that could happen to them at this point in their lives.

The eighty-year-old said, "I'd like nothing better than to have a good piss. I just stand there and it dribbles, and I have to go over and over again."

The eighty-five-year-old said, "I'd like nothing better than to have a good shit. I take every kind of laxative I can get my hands on, and it's still a problem."

The ninety-year-old man said, "Every morning at six A.M. sharp I have a good long piss, and a half hour later I have a fantastic shit. I'd like nothing better than to wake up before they happen."

● ● ●

OFFENSIVELY ETHNIC JOKES

● ● ● ● ● ● ●

What did the Polish mother say when her daughter said she was pregnant?

"Don't worry, honey. Maybe it's not yours."

• • •

Why couldn't the Polack get a job as the town idiot?

He was overqualified.

• • •

Hear about the Polish sky diver?

He was killed when his snorkel and flippers failed to open.

• • •

What is the most effective way to scare off a black mugger?

Threaten to wipe a booger on his new tennis shoes.

• • •

Hear about the black guy who suffered from insomnia?

He kept waking up every few days.

• • •

What do black men and sperm have in common?

Only one in two million does any work.

• • •

Why can't they cremate Irishmen?

Because it takes two weeks to put out the fire.

• • •

Where did the Irishman go for his vacation?

To a different bar.

• • •

What's three miles long and has an IQ of ten?

The St. Patrick's Day Parade.

• • •

Why did the Polack cross the road?

His dick was in a chicken.

• • •

Why did the chicken cross the road?

She was trying to get rid of the Polack.

• • •

Why wasn't the Polack worried when his car was stolen?

He got the license plate number.

• • •

What does a black kid get for his fourth birthday present?

A switchblade.

• • •

What does a black kid get for his eighteenth birthday present?

Bailed out.

• • •

An eighty-seven-year-old man goes to confession. "Bless me, Father, for I have sinned," the old duffer says.

"What is your confession?" the priest asks.

The old man says, "I cheated on my wife of sixty years with a twenty-one-year-old girl."

The priest is horrified. He says, "That's terrible. Tell me, I don't recognize your voice. Have you come to me before?"

"No," says the old man. "This is my first confession. Truth is, Father, I'm Jewish."

"Let me get this straight," the priest says. "You cheated on your wife with a twenty-one-year-old girl and you're Jewish. Why are you telling me this?"

"Hell," the old man says, "I'm telling everybody!"

• • •

What do you call six Arab women in a hot tub?

Gorillas in the mist.

• • •

What do you call an Arab with a goat under one arm and a sheep under the other?

Bisexual.

• • •

How does an Arab firing squad line up?

One behind the other.

• • •

Hear about the new Polish parachute?

It opens on impact.

• • •

How many Polacks does it take to take a bath?

Six—one to lie in the bathtub and five to spit on him.

• • •

What's the Polish definition of a washer-dryer?

A douche bag and a towel.

• • •

How many Italians does it take to change a light-bulb?

Four—one to steal it, one to change it, one to keep lookout, and one to shoot any witnesses.

• • •

How is an Italian hearse different from a regular one?

In an Italian hearse, the body is always in the trunk.

• • •

How can you tell if an Italian girl is old-fashioned?

She has a handlebar moustache.

• • •

What's black, three miles long, and smelly?

The line at the welfare office.

• • •

What word starts with N and ends with R that you never want to call a black man?

Neighbor.

• • •

How can you tell a bride at an Afghan wedding?

She's the one lying next to the groom.

• • •

How come there are no bars in Afghanistan?

They stay home and get bombed.

• • •

What's the latest fashion craze in Afghanistan?

Body bags by Gucci.

• • •

What's a Jewish-American princess's dream home?

Twenty rooms, thirty bathrooms, forty closets—no kitchen, no bedrooms.

• • •

What's a Jewish-American princess's favorite position?

Facing Bloomingdale's.

• • •

Why do Jewish-American princesses wear bikinis?

To separate the meat from the fish.

• • •

Hear about the Polish daredevil?

He jumped over twenty motorcycles in a school bus.

• • •

How does a Polish guy do crack?

He swipes his finger across his asshole and sniffs.

• • •

Why do they play sports on artificial turf in Poland?

To keep the cheerleaders from grazing.

• • •

An Arab was staggering through the Sahara Desert, desperate for water, when he saw something far off in the distance. Hoping to find water, he walked toward the image, only to find a little old Jewish man sitting at a card table with a bunch of neckties laid out on it.

The Arab asked, "Please, I'm dying of thirst. Can I have some water?"

The little old man replied, "I don't have any water, but why don't you buy a tie? Here's one that goes nicely—"

The Arab shouted, "I don't want a damn tie, you idiot! I need water!"

"Okay, already, so don't buy a tie. But to show you what a nice guy I am, I'll tell you that over that hill there, about four miles, is a nice restaurant. Walk that way; they'll give you all the water you want."

The Arab thanked him and walked away toward the hill and eventually disappeared. Three hours later the Arab came crawling back to where the man was sitting behind his card table.

The little Jewish merchant said, "I told you, about four miles. Couldn't you find it?"

The Arab said, "I found it all right, but your brother wouldn't let me in without a tie."

• • •

Why do white people throw their garbage away in clear plastic bags?

So Mexicans can go window shopping.

• • •

Why are there so few Mexican doctors?

It's hard to spray-paint a prescription.

• • •

89

What is the difference between American sewers and Mexican sewers?

Mexican sewers have diving boards.

• • •

How can you tell which guy coming to the orgy is Polish?

He's the one who shows up with an artificial vagina as his date.

• • •

Hear about the female tuna fish?

She smelled like a Polish woman.

• • •

Why was the Polack late for his own wedding?

He couldn't find a clean bowling shirt.

• • •

What comes out of the cake at a Scottish bachelor party?

A sheep in lingerie.

• • •

How can you tell if a kid is from Somalia?

His pet is a tapeworm.

• • •

What's so good about a blow job from an Ethiopian girl?

You know she'll swallow.

• • •

The Jewish mother answers the phone. "Hello?" she says.

The voice on the other end of the line says, "I want to rip your clothes off, tie you to the bed, and have sex with you ten different ways, then do it all over again!"

The Jewish mother replies, "All this you know from just saying hello?"

• • •

91

What's the difference between an Arab woman and an elephant?

A black veil and a moustache.

• • •

What do you call an Arab who chases garbage trucks?

The galloping gourmet.

• • •

Why were thermometers outlawed in Iran?

They caused brain damage.

• • •

Did you hear they came out with a new Oprah doll?

Ken and Barbie needed a maid.

• • •

How do black babies begin life?

As M&M-bryos.

• • •

Hear about the Million Man March in Washington, D.C.?

Four guys missed work.

• • •

How can you tell if a Vietnamese has burglarized your house?

Your cat's gone, and all your homework is done.

• • •

What do you call two Asians making love?

Fucking chinks.

• • •

What do you get when you cross a black guy and a Vietnamese?

Chocolate-chip Gookies.

• • •

A black guy goes to the ticket window at the Greyhound bus station. He says to the clerk, "Gimme a round-trip ticket."

The ticket clerk, who is white, asks him, "To where?"

"Ain't that just like a white man, always wantin' to know the black man's business," the black guy says. "It ain't none of your business where I'm going. Just gimme that ticket!"

• • •

Why did the schools stop teaching sex education in Iraq?

The sheep couldn't handle it.

• • •

What are the only three times a Puerto Rican sees a priest?

The day he gets baptized, the day he gets married, and the day he gets executed.

• • •

How can you tell if you have Puerto Ricans living in the house next to you?

Their cockroaches eat at Pizza Hut.

• • •

Two Polacks met, and one asked the other why he appeared so depressed.

"Because I just got back from taking my dog to obedience school," the first Polack says.

"Didn't your dog pass the course?" the second one asks.

"Sure," the first Polack says, "but he learned to sit up and roll over three days faster than I did."

• • •

How can you tell when the Mexicans have moved into your neighborhood?

The blacks start getting car insurance.

• • •

Who was the one man missing from the Million Man March?

The auctioneer.

• • •

What do you call a black hitchhiker?

Stranded.

• • •

Hear about the Polish antiabortion demonstration?

They picketed a coat-hanger factory.

• • •

Who are the two most famous women in real black history?

Aunt Jemima and Mutha Fuckah.

• • •

What do they call cocaine in Harlem?

Baby powder.

• • •

What's faster than a quarter rolling down a hill?

The Jew chasing after it.

• • •

What do you call a Jew wearing a gas mask?

A poor sport.

• • •

Why Jewish mothers don't drink:

Alcohol interferes with their suffering.

• • •

"I'd like the number for Mary Jones in Phoenix, Arizona," the black guy says to the 411 operator.

"There are multiple listings for Mary Jones in Phoenix, Arizona," the operator says. "Do you have a street name?"

The black guy hesitates a moment, then says, "Well, most people just call me Tyrone."

• • •

Two bowling teams, one Italian and one Polish, charter a double-decker bus; they're going to Las Vegas for the weekend. One team is in the bottom of the bus, and the other team is in the top of the bus. The Italians down below are whooping it up when one of them realizes he doesn't hear anything from the top. He walks up the stairs, and here are all the Polish guys from the second team clutching the seats in front of them with white knuckles, scared to death.

The Italian says, "What the heck's goin' on? We're down here havin' a grand old time."

One of the Polacks says, "Yeah, but you guys have a driver!"

• • •

Why don't Polacks like M&Ms?

They're too hard to peel.

• • •

A Polack walks into Dunkin' Donuts. He says, "Excuse me, miss . . . how many cups of coffee do you think this thermos will hold?"

She says, "I think it's a seven-cup thermos."

He says, "All right . . . give me two black, two with cream, and three with sugar."

• • •

Why do Mexicans always have tamales for Christmas dinner?

So they'll have something to unwrap!

• • •

What do you call two blacks sleeping together in a sleeping bag?

Twix!

• • •

How does a Russian commit suicide?

He smells his armpits.

• • •

A family of ducks is walking along the road when all of a sudden, a car swerves and kills all but one baby. Realizing that he doesn't yet know what he is, the baby duck wanders around looking for some answers. He sees a family of skunks walking in the same area that his family was, and what do you know—a car kills all but one of the babies, too. So the baby duck goes up to the baby skunk and says, "Do you know what I am?"

The skunk says, "Well, you're yellow; you have a beak, webbed feet, and feathers; so you must be a duck. Do you know what I am?"

The duck says, "Well, you're not quite white, not quite black; you smell like shit; so you must be a Mexican."

• • •

What do you call an Ethiopian with feathers glued on his ass?

A dart.

• • •

What do you call one hundred Ethiopians standing in shallow water?

Skinny dipping.

• • •

Why does a Doberman lick his balls?

To get the taste of Puerto Ricans out of his mouth.

• • •

TOP TEN REASONS WHY IT'S GOOD
TO BE ITALIAN

1. In-depth knowledge of bizarre pasta shapes.
2. Unembarrassed to wear fur.
3. No need to worry about tax returns.
4. Glorious military history . . . well, till about A.D. 400.
5. Can wear sunglasses inside.
6. Political stability.
7. Flexible working hours.
8. Live near the pope.
9. Can spend hours braiding girlfriend's armpit hair.
10. Sweating tenors.

• • •

What do you call two black guys on motorcycles in Los Angeles?

Chocolate ChiPs.

• • •

A German, a Frenchman, and a Jew were lost in the desert.

The German said, "I'm tired; I'm thirsty; I must have beer!"

The Frenchman said, "I'm tired; I'm thirsty; I must have wine!"

The Jew said, "I'm tired; I'm thirsty; I must have diabetes!"

• • •

What do you call a black dude with a job?

One in a million.

• • •

What is the difference between an Italian grand-mother and a Jewish grandmother?

The Italian grandmother says, "If you don't eat, I'll kill you."

The Jewish grandmother says, "If you don't eat, I'll kill myself."

• • •

How do you starve a black man?

Hide his food stamps in his work boots.

• • •

What do you call two Vietnamese in a Trans Am?

The Gooks of Hazard.

• • •

How do you drown a Haitian?

Give him a shoebox and tell him it floats.

• • •

What do you get when you cross a gay Eskimo and a black?

A snowblower that doesn't work.

• • •

What do you get when you cross a Mexican with an octopus?

I don't know, but it sure can pick tomatoes.

• • •

Why are Jewish men circumsized?

Jewish women don't want anything unless it's 20 percent off.

• • •

Pierre, a brave French fighter pilot, takes his girl-friend, Marie, out for a pleasant little picnic by the River Seine. It's a beautiful day, and love is in the air.

Marie leans over to Pierre and says, "Pierre, kiss me!"

Our hero grabs a bottle of merlot and splashes it on Marie's lips.

"What are you doing, Pierre?" says the startled Marie.

"I am Pierre the fighter pilot! When I have red meat, I have red wine!"

She smiles, and they start kissing.

When things began to heat up a little, Marie says, "Pierre, kiss me lower."

Our hero tears her blouse open, grabs a bottle of Chardonnay, and starts pouring it all over her tits.

"Pierre! What are you doing?" asks the bewildered Marie.

"I am Pierre the fighter pilot! When I have white meat, I have white wine!"

They resume their passionate interlude, and things really steam up. Marie leans close to his ear and whispers, "Pierre, kiss me lower!"

Pierre rips off her underwear, grabs a bottle of cognac, and pours it in her lap. He then strikes a match and lights it on fire.

Marie shrieks and dives into the river. Standing waist-deep, Marie throws her arms up and screams furiously, "PIERRE, WHAT IN THE HELL DO YOU THINK YOU'RE DOING?"

Pierre stands up and says, "I am Pierre the fighter pilot! If I go down, I go down in flames!"

• • •

Have you seen the newest Jewish-American princess horror movie?

Debbie Does Dishes.

• • •

What is the best way to stop an Iraqi tank attack?

Shoot the soldiers who are pushing them.

• • •

What should you do if you see a black jogger?

Trip him and give the lady's purse back to her.

• • •

Why do all Jews have double-paned windows on their houses?

So their kids can't hear the ice cream trucks.

• • •

What do you get when you cross a pit bull with a redneck?

An all-white neighborhood.

• • •

What do you get when you cross a Korean chef and a French poodle?

Dinner.

• • •

What do you call a Mexican female who has no legs?

Cuntsuelo.

• • •

What are the first four words every Puerto Rican child must learn?

"Give me your wallet!"

• • •

How can you spot an Italian woman in a cow pasture?

She's the one without a bell.

• • •

How can you tell that a Polack has wandered into the forest?

All the bears are lighting fires to drive him back out.

• • •

How does a romance novel in Harlem end?

The hero gets the heroin.

• • •

What is a Jewish-American princess's definition of a ménage à trois?

Two headaches and a hard-on.

• • •

What term describes raping a Jewish-American princess?

Raiding the ice box.

• • •

How can you tell if a Polack has been drinking from the toilet?

His breath smells better.

• • •

Why don't many black guys write books?

Because it takes them ten years to finish a sentence.

• • •

GROSS AND GROSSER

● ● ● ● ● ● ●

Why do blondes insist on guys wearing condoms?

So they'll have a doggie bag for later.

• • •

A class, somewhere in the United States . . .

It was English class, and Johnny was sitting in his desk with an embarrassed look on his face. The teacher was asking children if they could give an example of a sentence with the word *definitely* in it. Finally, she asked Johnny.

Johnny smiled, sweat running down his forehead.

"Do farts have lumps?" he asked.

The teacher replied, "No."

Johnny slumped down in his chair and replied, "Then I *definitely* just shit myself."

• • •

What's the definition of necrophilia?

Never having to say you're sorry.

• • •

Why haven't they cremated Colonel Sanders yet?

They haven't decided on regular or extra crispy.

• • •

Why does Helen Keller have only one hand?

She tried to read a stop sign at 55 mph.

• • •

What do you do when the dishwasher breaks down?

Slap the bitch and tell her to get back to work.

• • •

How did Helen Keller burn her ear?

She answered the iron.

How did she burn the other ear?

The guy called back.

• • •

How can you tell if a valentine is from a leper?

The tongue's still in the envelope.

• • •

Why did God put long legs on women?

To keep their feet from smelling like fish.

• • •

How do you get a man to eat shit?

Wipe forward.

• • •

What's grosser then gross?

Siamese twins joined at the mouth, and one of them throwing up.

• • •

Why wasn't JFK a good boxer?

He couldn't take a shot to the head.

• • •

Walking into the bar, Harvey said to the bartender, "Pour me a stiff one, Joe Bob. I just had another fight with the little woman."

"Oh, yeah?" Joe Bob asked. "And how did this one end?"

"When it was over," Harvey replied, "she came to me on her hands and knees."

"Really? Now that's a switch! What did she say?"

"She said, 'Come out from under that bed, you gutless weasel!'"

• • •

A man is having problems with his dick, which certainly had seen better times. He consults a doctor who, after a couple of tests, says, "Sorry, but you've overdone it the last thirty years. Your dick is burned out; you have only thirty erections left in your penis."

The man walks home, deeply depressed. His wife is waiting for him at the front door and asks him what the doctor said concerning his problem. He tells her what the doc told him.

She says, "Oh, no, only thirty times! We shouldn't waste any of them—we should make a list!"

He replies, "I already made a list on the way home. Sorry, your name isn't on it."

• • •

WHAT ARE THE FIVE LEVELS OF SEX?

1. Smurf Sex: This happens during the honeymoon; you both keep doing it until you're blue in the face.
2. Kitchen Sex: This is at the beginning of the marriage; you'll have sex anywhere, including the kitchen.
3. Bedroom Sex: You've calmed down a bit, perhaps have kids, so you've got to do it in the bedroom.
4. Hallway Sex: This is where you pass each other in the hallway and say, "Fuck you!"
5. Courtroom Sex: This is when you get divorced and your wife fucks you in front of everyone in the courtroom.

• • •

Storming into his lawyer's office, a Texas oil magnate demanded that divorce proceedings begin at once against his young bride.

"What's the problem?" the lawyer asked.

"I want to hit that adulterin' bitch for breach of contract," snapped the oilman.

"I don't know if that will fly," said the lawyer. "I mean, your wife isn't a piece of property; you don't own her!"

"Damn right," the tycoon rejoined, "but I sure as hell expect exclusive drillin' rights!"

• • •

As a painless way to save money, a young couple arranged that every time they had sex, the husband would put his pocket change into a porcelain piggy bank on the bedside table.

One night, while being unusually athletic, he accidentally knocked the bank to the floor, where it smashed into pieces. To his surprise, among the masses of coins, there were handfuls of five- and ten-dollar bills.

He asked his wife what was up.

"Well," she replied, "not everyone is as cheap as you are."

• • •

A married guy was out getting a little "strange stuff" with a woman who was not his wife, when he suffered a massive heart attack and died.

The undertaker called his wife as he was preparing the body, saying, "Your late husband died with a tremendous erection that we can't get to go away. . . . What would you like us to do?"

She replied, "Somehow, that doesn't surprise me. Cut it off and stuff it up his ass."

The next day, when she went to view the body, she noticed a somewhat pained expression on her deceased husband's face as he lay in the casket.

Bending over him, she said, "Hurts, doesn't it?"

• • •

A man and his son were walking through a field and saw two dogs mating.

The little boy asked, "What are those dogs doing?"

The father replied, "Well, son, they're making a puppy."

The following evening, the little boy was thirsty, so he went from his bed to get a glass of water. Not being able to reach the glasses, he walked unannounced into his parents' bedroom, who were making love in their usual missionary position.

Confused, the boy asked what they were doing.

The father responded, "Well, son, we are making you a little brother."

The little boy replied, "Please turn Mom over, Dad, I'd rather have a puppy!"

• • •

What do you call a redneck who has a dog and a cat?

A switch-hitter.

• • •

A little old lady goes to the doctor and says, "Doctor, I have this problem with gas, but it really doesn't bother me too much. They never smell and are always silent. In fact, I've farted at least twenty times since I've been here in your office. You didn't know I was farting, because they didn't smell and are silent."

The doctor says, "I see. Take these pills and come back and see me next week."

The next week the lady goes back to the doctor. "Doctor," she says, "I don't know what the hell you gave me, but now my farts are still silent, but they really stink."

"Good," the doctor said. "Now that we've cleared up your sinuses, let's work on your hearing."

• • •

What did one butt cheek say to the other cheek?

"If we stick together we can stop this shit!"

• • •

How do you know that diarrhea is hereditary?

It runs in your jeans.

• • •

What is worse than a one-inch penis?

Nothing.

• • •

How many animals can you put in a pair of panty-hose?

One ass, one beaver, a whole bunch of hares, two calves, and a fish nobody can find!

• • •

What do you call a vegetarian with diarrhea?

A salad shooter.

• • •

What do you call a gay man's scrotum?

Mud flaps.

• • •

What do a blonde and a pirate have in common?

They both have black patches.

• • •

How do you get a blonde to cross her legs?

Tell her that her shoes are on the wrong feet.

• • •

What do you call a blonde with two brain cells?

Pregnant.

• • •

This guy walks into a small town bar and orders a drink from the bartender.

The bartender delivers his drink and shouts out to the bar patrons, "Forty-six!" Everyone starts to laugh. Then he shouts out, "Thirty-nine!" Now the patrons laugh even louder.

The visitor is curious, so he asks the bartender, "What is going on?"

The bartender says, "This is a small town, with small, impressionable children, and so we decided to put numbers to our dirty jokes instead of saying them."

The visitor is astounded. "Let me try!" he says. He shouts, "Forty-six!" Nothing happens. He shouts, "Thirty-nine!" Still nothing happens.

The visitor says to the bartender, "I don't understand. I used exactly the same numbers you did, and nothing happened!"

The bartender replies, "Well, some folks can tell a joke, and some folks can't."

• • •

Signs She's Getting Bored Having Sex with You:

When you request sex, she replies, "Wait till the NyQuil kicks in."

Gets very upset when the ashtray falls off your ass.

Actually answers when you ask, "Who's your daddy?"

Only moans during commercial breaks.

Keeps trying to set you up with her friends.

Runs for vacant Senate seat in New York.

Keeps asking, "Are you SURE you're not gay?"

Holds up a picture of the *Playboy* centerfold to hurry you along.

Asks to be on top so she can balance her checkbook more easily.

Bangs her head on the headboard BEFORE you begin.

Starts her fake orgasms during foreplay.

• • •

A couple gets married, and the wife puts a foot-locker in the bedroom. She locks it, then puts the only key on a chain around her neck. For fifty years, her husband tries to figure out what's in there, but she always changes the subject and avoids the issue.

Finally, on the night of their fiftieth wedding anniversary, he says to her, "I've got to know what's in the trunk!"

She takes the key and unlocks the foot locker, and inside are two ears of corn and $25,000.

The guy says, "What's with the two ears of corn?"

She says, "Well, umm, in the fifty years, every time I broke our marriage vows, I put an ear of corn in the trunk."

The guy figures, "Twice in fifty years—not so bad . . ." Then he says, "And what's the $25,000?"

She says, "Well, every time I got a bushel, I sold it."

• • •

What has four legs and one arm?

A happy pit bull.

• • •

FIVE THINGS YOU SHOULD NEVER SAY
IN A MEN'S ROOM

1. "Interesting . . . more floaters than sinkers."
2. "I've never seen that color before."
3. "Damn, this water's cold."
4. "Boy, that sure looks like a maggot."
5. "Whew! Who died?"

• • •

Little Johnny is late to class one day, and the teacher asks him where he has been.

He replies, "I've been down by the creek sticking cherry bombs up frogs' asses."

"You mean rectum," corrected the teacher.

"Wrecked 'em?" says Little Johnny. "I fuckin' *killed* 'em!!"

• • •

Did you hear about the constipated Wheel of Fortune player?

He wanted to buy a bowel.

• • •

Well, did you hear about the constipated accountant?

He couldn't budget.

Did you hear about the constipated composer?

He couldn't finish the last movement.

Did you hear about the constipated mathematician?

He worked it out with a pencil.

• • •

A stuffy matron is with a new man in a top restaurant. The onion soup gets to her, and as the waiter is serving the main dishes, she lets loose a bombastic fart. Trying to save face, she says to the waiter, "Sir! Please stop that immediately."

"Certainly, madam," replies the waiter. "Which way was it headed?"

• • •

Two old women were sitting on a bench waiting for their bus. The buses were running late, and a lot of time passed. Finally, one woman turned to the other and said, "You know, I've been sitting here so long, my butt fell asleep!"

The other woman turned to her and said, "I know! I heard it snoring!"

• • •

TEN THINGS NEVER TO SAY TO A GUY WITH A SMALL DICK

1. Why don't we just cuddle?
2. Make it dance.
3. Wow, and your feet are so big.
4. My last boyfriend was four inches bigger.
5. My eight-year-old brother has one like that.
6. How sweet, you brought incense.
7. Maybe if we water it, it'll grow.
8. Have you ever thought of working in a sideshow?
9. I didn't know they came that small.
10. Why is God punishing you?

• • •

TEN SIGNS THAT YOU DRINK TOO MUCH

1. The back of your head keeps getting hit by the toilet seat.
2. You lose arguments with inanimate objects.
3. You can focus better with one eye closed.
4. Boris Yeltsin calls personally to ask you to slow down on the vodka.
5. Worried friends call Monday morning to make sure you returned the goat.
6. You fart and then feel a lump in your back pocket.
7. You don't recognize your wife unless seen through the bottom of a glass.
8. That damned pink elephant followed you home again.
9. You have to hold on to the lawn to keep from falling off the earth.
10. You fall off the floor.

• • •

TEN SIGNS THAT THE ROMANCE IS GONE

1. You let one rip in your sleep and don't care if she hears.
2. He yawns when you bitch about that guy hitting on you at work.
3. Talking dirty in bed means shouting obscenities when she hogs the blanket.
4. Her PMS lasts all month.
5. When he lends you five bucks, he expects it back.
6. Two weeks, no orgasm.
7. Three weeks no orgasm . . . and you still don't miss it.
8. She's using your toothbrush to scrub the toilet.
9. The only thigh you see on your anniversary is at KFC.
10. She's keeping a list of things she'll do after you're finally dead.

• • •

A young dating couple was driving down the road in a very busy area when things started to get somewhat passionate. So they decided to pull over to park and have some fun.

Things were really getting hot, and they were not paying any attention to what was going on outside.

All of a sudden a policeman was tapping on their window.

The cop could hardly contain himself. "Didn't you know that you are not supposed to be having sex on a public roadway?" he asked the couple. Being embarrassed at getting caught, they said yes and apologized.

"Well," he said, "I will have to write you a ticket."

So the cop wrote the ticket and reminded them next time to watch their behavior.

After getting dressed, the girlfriend asked her boyfriend what the policeman wrote the ticket for.

He responded, "Doing 69 in a 35 mph speed zone!"

• • •

A guy met a girl in a bar and asked, "May I buy you a drink?"

She replied, "Okay, but it won't do you any good."

A little later, he asked, "May I buy you another drink?"

Again she replied, "Okay, but it won't do you any good."

He invited her up to his apartment, and she replied, yet again, "Okay, but it won't do you any good."

They got to his apartment, and he said, "You are the most beautiful woman I have ever seen. I want you for my wife."

She replied, "Oh, that's different. Send her in."

• • •

The young lady admired the watch in the store window every time she walked by.

She finally entered the shop one day and said, "Just how much is that watch?"

"It's two thousand dollars, ma'am," said the guy behind the counter.

"Hmmm. Well, would you consider time payments for it?" asked the lady.

"Just what sort of time schedule did you have in mind?" inquired the guy.

The young lady replied, "I was thinking two times a week for the next two months."

● ● ●

In a small town in Tennessee, Big Bubba decides it's time for his son, fourteen-year-old Billy Bob, to learn the facts of life. He takes him to the local house of ill repute, which is fronted by a beauty parlor. Bubba introduces Billy Bob to the madam and explains that it's time for his indoctrination to sex.

The madam says, "Bubba, you've been such a good customer over the years, I'm going to see to this personally."

So the madam takes Billy Bob by the hand and

leads him upstairs, where she completes his deflowering.

Later, as they are walking downstairs, the madam says, "Since this is your first time, I'm going to see that you get the full treatment before you leave; I'm going to give you a manicure."

Two weeks later Bubba and Billy Bob run into the madam on the main street.

Billy Bob is acting a little shy, so the madam smiles and says, "Well, Billy Bob, don't you remember me?"

"Yes, ma'am," the boy stammers, "You're the lady that gave me the crabs and then cut off my fingernails so I couldn't scratch 'em."

• • •

"Oh, Mom," sobbed Little Mary, "I'm pregnant!"

"What!? How could you?" screamed the mother. "And just who is the father?"

The daughter lifted up her tearful face and wailed, "How should I know? You're the one who would never let me go steady!"

• • •

Maw is outside the house hanging up the laundry, when she hears Paw in the kitchen. Maw walks in and says, "Paw, get out there and fix that there outhouse."

Paw says, "All right, Maw." Paw walks out to the outhouse, looks at it, and says, "Maw, there ain't nothin' wrong with this here outhouse!"

Maw says, "Yes, there is. Put your head down in the hole."

Paw puts his head down in the hole, and he says, "Maw, there ain't nothin' wrong with this here outhouse!"

Maw says, "Now, pull your head out of the hole."

Paw goes to lift up his head, and he says, "Oww! OWW! Maw! MAW! My beard's stuck in the cracks in the seat!"

Maw says, "Aggravatin', ain't it?"

• • •

A state trooper notices a car weaving in the road, and when he pulls it over, a beautiful woman gets out.

She is clearly under the influence, but just to make sure, he gives her the Breathalyzer test.

Sure enough, she's over the limit, so the trooper says, "Madam, you've had a couple of stiff ones."

"Oh," says the lady, "it shows THAT, too?"

• • •

There was this couple that was married for twenty years, and every time they made love, the husband always insisted on shutting off the lights. Well, after twenty years, the wife felt this was stupid. She figured she would break him of the crazy habit. So one night, while they were in the middle of a romantic session, she turned on the lights. She looked down and saw that her husband was holding a battery-operated pleasure device.

She gets completely upset. "You impotent bastard!" she screamed at him. "How could you be lying to me all of these years? You better explain yourself!"

The husband looks at her straight in the eyes and says calmly, "I'll explain the toy if you explain the kids."

• • •

A woman was shaking out a rug on the balcony of her seventeenth-floor condominium when a sudden gust of wind blew her over the railing.

"Damn, that was stupid," she thought as she fell. "What a way to die."

As she passed the fourteenth floor, a man standing at his railing caught her in his arms. While she looked at him in disbelieving gratitude, he asked, "Do you suck?"

"No!" she shrieked, aghast. So he dropped her.

As she passed the twelfth floor, another man reached out and caught her.

"Do you screw?" he asked.

"Of course not!" she exclaimed before she could stop herself. He dropped her, too.

The poor woman prayed to God for one more chance. As luck would have it, she was caught a third time, by a man on the eighth floor.

"I suck! I screw!" she screamed in panic.

"Slut!" he said, and dropped her.

• • •

What is the difference between a blonde and a bowling ball?

You can only get three fingers in a bowling ball.

• • •

GROSS CELEBRITY JOKES

● ● ● ● ● ● ●

What was the temperature of Martha's Vineyard after JFK Jr.'s plane went down?

Three below.

• • •

Where do the Kennedys go for their vacation?

All over Martha's Vineyard.

• • •

What do the Kennedys miss most about Martha's Vineyard?

The runway.

• • •

George W. Bush is spending his first night in the White House. The ghost of George Washington appears, and George W. says, "How can I best serve my country?"

Washington says, "Never tell a lie."

The next night, the ghost of Thomas Jefferson appears. George W. says, "How can I best serve my country?"

Jefferson says, "Listen to the people."

On the third night, the ghost of Abe Lincoln appears. George W. says, "How can I best serve my country?"

Lincoln says, "Go to the theater."

• • •

What's the primary difference between Madonna and the Statue of Liberty?

The statue was made by the French, Madonna Frenched her maid.

• • •

How do hookers clean their teeth in Los Angeles?

With dental Fleiss.

• • •

What was the last thing that went through Kurt Cobain's mind when he shot himself?

The roof of his mouth.

• • •

Hillary Clinton and Janet Reno were having one of those girl-to-girl talks, and Hillary said to Janet, "You're lucky that you don't have to put up with men having sex with you. I have to put up with Bill, and there is no telling where he last had his pecker."

Janet responded, "Just because I am ugly doesn't mean I don't have to fight off unwelcome sexual advances."

Hillary asked, "Well, how do you deal with the problem?"

"Whenever I feel that a guy is getting ready to make a pass at me, I muster all my might and squeeze out the loudest, nastiest fart that I can."

That night, Bill was already in bed with the lights out when Hillary slipped into bed. She could hear him start to stir and knew that he would be wanting some action. She had been saving her farts all day, and she was ready for him. She tensed up her butt cheeks and forced out the most disgusting-sounding fart you could imagine. Bill rolled over and asked, "Janet, is that you?"

• • •

Why was JFK Jr. flying to Martha's Vineyard?

He wanted to crash his cousin's wedding.

• • •

Why didn't the wedding guests at Hyannisport want JFK Jr. to show up?

He was a complete wreck.

• • •

Did you hear about the new Marilyn Monroe stamp?

When you lick it, you feel like one of the Kennedys.

• • •

Why doesn't Ronald Reagan use Viagra?

Because it'd be like putting a new flagpole on a condemned building.

• • •

Which has more fingerprints—the FBI or the PLA?

The PLA (Pamela Lee's Ass).

• • •

Why did Rosa Parks really refuse to move to the back of the bus?

She was just too damn lazy.

• • •

What two people were shot in a theater?

Abraham Lincoln, and the guy sitting in front of Pee Wee Herman.

• • •

What's black, seven feet tall, and cleans hotel rooms?

Wilt Chambermaid.

• • •

What do O. J. and fireworks have in common?

Both have killed in the past, but they still get let off.

• • •

What did O. J. say when someone finally asked him where he was between nine and eleven?

Second grade.

• • •

What do Hillary Clinton and J. Edgar Hoover have in common?

They're both female impersonators.

• • •

During a recent staff meeting in heaven, God, Moses, and Saint Peter concluded that the behavior of politicians such as former President Bill Clinton and Congressman Gary Condit had brought about the need for an Eleventh Commandment. They worked long and hard in a brainstorming session to try to settle on the wording of the new commandment, because they realized that it should have the same majesty and dignity as the other ten.

After many revisions they finally agreed that the Eleventh Commandment should be, *Thou shalt not comfort thy rod with thy staff.*

• • •

What's the difference between Gary Condit and the Afghan army?

Gary Condit has at least one confirmed kill.

• • •

Did you hear there are two suspects in Chris Farley's death?

Ben and Jerry.

• • •

Did you hear Elton John's songs about Chris Farley?

Don't Let the Worms Bore Down On Me
Saturday Night's All Gone for Me
Farley in the Wind
Good-bye Rocky Road
Guess That's Why I'm Turning Blue
I'm Not Standing

• • •

What did Chris Farley call out whenever he saw a school bus?

"Hey! Stop that Twinkie!"

What did Chris say when he got on the school bus?

"Hey, where's the cream filling!"

• • •

Did you hear about the next Peanuts TV special?

"You're a Dead Man, Charlie Brown!"

• • •

What's the difference between Roy Rogers and Phil Hartman?

Trigger had nothing to do with Roy Rogers's death.

• • •

What's Roy Rogers's new theme song?

"Happy Snails to You . . ."

• • •

What did Ted Kennedy say to Mary Jo Kopechne when she asked him if he was going to leave his wife for her?

"We'll cross that bridge when we come to it."

• • •

Why did it take Ted so long to report the drowning at Chappaquiddick?

It took him several dives to get Mary Jo's clothes back on.

• • •

What's the difference between Ted Kennedy and Joey Buttafuco?

Joey's Mary Jo is still alive.

• • •

What were Marilyn Monroe's last words?

"Bobby, are you sure these are aspirins?"

• • •

Did you hear that JFK Jr. just hired a new copilot?

Jacques Cousteau.

• • •

What's the difference between JFK and Bill Clinton?

One had his head blown off in the back of a limousine, and the other was assassinated.

• • •

How did Rock Hudson's doctor reassure him?

He told Rock, "Don't worry, we'll have you back on your knees in no time."

• • •

Why did they bury Rock Hudson face down?

So his friends could drop over for a cold one.

• • •

What was Rock Hudson's first sign that he had AIDS?

A pounding in the ass.

• • •

How did AIDS spread across the country?

In the rear end of an old Hudson.

• • •

What did Sammy Davis Jr. say to Rock Hudson when he got to Heaven?

"If you smoke 'em or poke 'em, those butts will kill you every time!"

• • •

What was Rock Hudson's favorite meal?

Tube steak smothered in underwear.

• • •

Where does a jogger go to pick his nose?

The Green Mile.

• • •

How does James Bond like his pussy?

Shaven, not furred.

• • •

How does Sinead O'Connor part her hair?

She squats.

• • •

What did Ted Bundy get for Christmas?

A smoking jacket.

• • •

What is a Ted Bundy sandwich?

Fried egg on burnt toast.

• • •

Did you hear about Ted Bundy's last meal?

In the morning he got bacon, eggs, and toast. Later on that same day, he got the juice.

• • •

What were Tammy Wynette's last words to her husband?

"Stand by your hand."

• • •

What do Kurt Cobain and Michelangelo have in common?

They both used their brains to paint the ceiling.

• • •

Did you hear about the Kentucky Fried Chicken location in New York?

The special was called a "Bucket of Hillary"—two small breasts, two large thighs, and a bunch of left wings.

• • •

Did you hear Monica Lewinsky is now working for 7-11?

She's endorsing the Big Gulp.

• • •

Why is Clinton so interested in events in the Middle East?

He thinks the Gaza Strip is a topless bar.

• • •

What was Clinton's Secret Service code name?

Unibanger.

• • •

How did Bill Clinton reply regarding questions of "coaching" Monica Lewinsky's testimony?

"It wasn't words that I put in her mouth."

• • •

Why was Clinton's approval rating so high?

Because Monica was taking the pole.

What was the press name for the presidential scandal?

Fornigate.

• • •

What position did Monica Lewinsky have at the White House?

Missionary.

• • •

What does Monica Lewinsky have on her resume?

"Sat on the presidential staff."

• • •

If Kenneth Starr extended his probe, what was wrong with Clinton doing the same?

• • •

Bill: "I didn't lie in the DEPOSITION. . . . I told her to lie in THAT there position."

• • •

The President got a dog so that Hillary wouldn't be confused when she walked past the Oval Office and heard, "Roll over. Sit. Stay. Good. Now here's your bone."

• • •

Did you hear Clinton wanted to declare a new National Bird?

The spread eagle.

• • •

What is the difference between Monica Lewinsky and a Hoover vacuum cleaner?

Where the dirtbag attaches.

• • •

How many White House interns does it take to screw in a lightbulb?

None—they're too busy screwing the president.

• • •

What's Clinton's favorite card game?

Poker.

• • •

How did they finally bust Clinton?

Monica coughed up the evidence.

• • •

Most people worry about getting AIDS from sex. Bill Clinton worried about getting sex from aides!

• • •

What was Slick Willie's other nickname?

The President-erect.

• • •

What's President Clinton's nickname for Hillary?

My Little Buttercup.

For Monica?

My Little Suction Cup.

• • •

What's the difference between Osama Bin Laden and a bag of shit?

The bag.

• • •

What's the definition of "mixed emotions?"

Seeing Bin Laden go over a cliff in your new Corvette.

• • •

Osama bin Laden, not feeling well and concerned about his mortality, goes to consult a psychic about the date of his death.

Closing her eyes and silently reaching into the realm of the future, she finds the answer. "You will die on an American holiday."

"Which one?" Osama bin Laden asks nervously.

"It doesn't matter," the psychic says. "Whenever you die, it will be an American holiday."

• • •

SO GROSS EVEN WE WERE OFFENDED

• • • • • • •

What do lesbians use for lubricant?

Tartar sauce!

• • •

What's the difference between a fag and a sup-pository?

None!

• • •

What do you call a gay black man?

A bruthafucker!

• • •

What's white and crawls up your ass?

Uncle Ben's Perverted Rice!

• • •

Why did the fag get fired from his job at the sperm bank?

He was caught drinking on the job!

• • •

A guy walks in and sits down at a bar. The side of his face is bruised and bleeding, so the bartender asks, "What in the world happened to you, buddy?"

The guy says, "Oh, I got in a fight with my girlfriend, and I called her a two-bit whore."

"Yeah?" asks the bartender. "What did she do?"

"She hit me with her bag of quarters."

• • •

What do you call ground-up glass in a condom?

An organ grinder!

• • •

How can a woman tell when it is time to stop breast-feeding her son?

When he starts selling meal tickets to his friends.

• • •

A man stops into this little backwoods restaurant for lunch, and after finishing his meal he inquires the way to the rest room. He's told that it's around the back of the building, so he heads through the back door, finds the outhouse, and takes a shit, only to discover there's no toilet paper. But there is a sign on the wall that reads, *Wipe yourself with your finger; then insert the finger into this hole, and your finger will be cleaned with great attention.*

So the man wipes up and sticks his finger through the hole. On the other side is standing a little boy, holding a brick in either hand. He claps them together at the sight of the finger poking through. The guy screams in pain, yanks his hand back, and starts sucking on his finger.

• • •

What is another name for homos with AIDS?

Tool-and-die workers.

• • •

What are the three reasons that make anal sex better than vaginal sex?

It's warmer, it's tighter, and it's degrading to women.

• • •

A guy says to his wife, "I'm in the mood for some sixty-nine." She says, "It's that time of the month, but if you don't care, I don't care." They go into the bedroom, and are sixty-nining like mad dogs when the doorbell rings. She says, "Answer the door." He says, "But my face is a mess." She says, "It's just the mailman. Answer the door, and if he says anything, just tell him you were eating a jam sandwich."

He opens the door and says, "I'm sorry about my mouth; I was eating a jam sandwich." The mailman says, "I wasn't looking at the jam on your mouth; I was looking at the peanut butter on your forehead."

• • •

What do you say to a blonde with no arms and no legs?

"Nice tits!"

• • •

What's the difference between sushi and pussy?

Rice.

• • •

What did the blind, deaf, dumb, black quadriplegic spastic get for Christmas?

Cancer.

• • •

What's grosser than having your girlfriend pass you her gum while you French kiss her?

When she tells you it wasn't gum.

• • •

Why did God give women yeast infections?

So they would learn what it's like to live with an irritating cunt.

• • •

What stops a woman's guts from falling out of her vagina?

The vacuum in her head.

• • •

Did you hear about the guy who's a dyslexic bulemic?

He eats, and then he sticks his finger up his ass.

• • •

How can you tell if a girl's pussy lips are really swollen?

When the crotch of her panties looks like Jiffy Pop.

• • •

A taxi driver goes to a bar to pick up his fare, a really drunk guy who has been in the bar way too long. After giving directions back to his house, he and the taxi driver are talking.

The drunk guy leans forward and says, "Hey, taxi dude! Think you got enough room in the front for a case of beer and a couple of burgers?"

Taxi guy says "Sure! Not a problem."

The drunk guy goes, *"BLLEEECCCHHHHH."*

• • •

What do women and shrimp have in common?

The pink part is pretty good, and they're more enjoyable with their heads cut off.

• • •

What is a redneck's definition of meat that is well done?

Cooked long enough so that the tire marks have all disappeared.

• • •

A couple's taking a walk, and as they walk hand in hand, the guy starts to get aroused. He's just about to get frisky when she says, "I hope you don't mind, but I have to take a pee."

He says, "Sure, go behind the hedge."

She disappears behind the hedge, and as he waits, he hears the sound of her jeans being rolled down her legs and imagines her exposed twat. He can't contain himself, so he reaches through a gap in the hedge and touches her leg. Then he moves his hand up her thigh until he finds himself gripping something long and thick between her legs.

He says, "My God, Mary, did you change your sex?"

She says, "No, I changed my mind. I'm taking a shit instead."

• • •

What should you do to your girlfriend when she is bad and forgets her birth control pill?

Give her a good tongue-lashing.

• • •

Why won't Charlie the Tuna eat his old lady?

She smells like people.

• • •

A boy comes to his father and asks, "Dad, what does a vagina look like?"

"Well, son," the father says, "before sex it looks like a perfect pink rosebud with a sweet perfume."

"So," asks the kid, "what does it look like after sex?"

"Well, son, have you ever seen a bulldog eating mayonnaise?"

• • •

What do a blonde and a Harley have in common?

It takes ten to fifteen minutes of messing with them to get a good ride, and when you stand them up, they leak.

• • •

Why are men so concerned about the size of their penises?

Because they should be.

• • •

How do you know that you've had a good blow job?

You have to burp her to get your balls back.

• • •

A newly married couple was walking along in their village along a winding country road. The husband had been trying to figure out a way to approach his new wife for sex, since they hadn't screwed yet and the sexual tension was beginning to be more than he could handle. As they walked, they came across a cow and a bull engaged in the act of reproduction.

The husband leaned over to his new bride and whispered in her ear, "Darling, would you like me to do what the bull is doing?"

"Do what you want," she said, "but don't be too rough—she isn't one of our cows."

• • •

How can you tell if a whore is genuinely elegant?

She uses lipstick on all of her VD sores.

• • •

What is the leading cause of death among lesbians?

Hair balls.

• • •

Little Timmy was in the garden, filling in a hole, when his neighbor peered over the fence. Interested in what the kid was up to, he politely asked, "What are you up to there, Timmy?"

"My goldfish died, "Timmy said without looking up, "and I've just buried him."

The neighbor said, "Why such a big hole for a goldfish?"

Timmy patted down the last heap of earth, then replied, "Because he's inside your fucking cat."

• • •

How can you tell when a girl is too fat to fuck?

When you pull down her pants, and her pussy is still in them.

• • •

Why don't blondes in San Francisco wear black miniskirts?

Because their balls will show.

• • •

What is the ideal weight for every lawyer?

Three pounds, including the urn.

• • •

Why do gay guys prefer rubbers with ridges?

Better traction in the mud.

• • •

How can you tell that the woman you're dating is promiscuous?

Her pussy lips are so loose she has to tuck them in to wear a miniskirt.

• • •

What do you call a gay masochist?

A cocksucker for punishment.

• • •

Gregory hasn't taken a crap in two weeks, so the doctor gives him some powerful laxatives and admits him to the hospital. In the middle of the night, Gregory lets loose all over the sheets, the bed, and the floor. He's so embarrassed that he rolls up the sheets and throws them out the window.

Two winos are sleeping it off under the hospital window when the mess hits the first one. The guy starts flailing around until he wrestles the sheet off of him.

His buddy says, "What the hell's going on?"

The first guy says, "I think I just beat the shit out of a ghost."

• • •

A young, serious babe escorting her ugly old aunt to the doctor told him, "We're here for a routine examination."

"Very well, my dear," he answered. "Go behind that curtain over there and remove all of your clothes."

"Oh, the examination is not for me; it's for old Auntie here!"

"Well, in that case," he countered, "madam, please stick out your tongue."

• • •

You Might Be a Redneck If:

You think *Volvo* is part of a woman's anatomy.
You consider your license plate customized because it was made by your father.

• • •

How do you know if you've walked into a lesbian bar?

There are no balls on the pool table, and all the cues are sticky.

• • •

<u>Top Euphemisms for Masturbating</u>:

    Lap-based Web browsing.
    Getting some air nookie.
    Wrangling the serpent.
    Shaking your fist at your ex-girlfriend.
    Releasing the hostages.
    Tickling your Elmo.
    Downloading from your own Web site.
    Evicting the testicular squatters.

● ● ●

Why do blondes take the pill?

Just so they know what day of the week it is.

● ● ●

How can you tell when a blonde's been in your re-frigerator?

There is lipstick on your cucumbers.

● ● ●

How do you get a girl from Arkansas into an elevator?

First grease up the doorway; then throw in a Twinkie.

• • •

What's the smartest thing to say to a woman?

"Tell me now before I blow twenty bucks on drinks."

• • •

A small company was on the edge of bankruptcy. The owner summoned his two-man sales force into his office.

"Things aren't going too well, guys," he announced grimly. "So to perk up sales I'm announcing a contest. The guy with the most sales gets a blow job."

"What does the loser get?" asked one of the salesmen.

The owner looked at both men and said, "The loser gets to give it."

• • •

Why do women have orgasms?

It gives them one extra reason to moan.

• • •

How can you tell if your date is really ugly?

You take her to dinner. When the waiter comes, he puts her plate on the floor.

• • •

How can a faggot prevent AIDS?

He can sit tight and keep his mouth shut.

• • •

What's black and blue and hates sex?

A rape victim.

• • •

What do you throw a drowning lawyer?

His partners.

• • •

What is definitely gross?

While you are fucking some broad, her tapeworm gives you head.

• • •

What do you call a girls' soccer team when they are all having their periods?

The Red Socks.

• • •

How can a redneck tell if he had a good time at the party last night?

He wakes up in a pool of his own puke.

• • •

What do you get when you have a group of women with PMS and yeast infections?

A whine and cheese convention.

• • •

What advantage did the abortionist who was also a cannibal have?

He never had to go out for lunch.

• • •

What do you call a Playboy centerfold who's a lesbian?

Bitch.

• • •

Why do men want to vote for a female for president?

Because we'd only have to pay her half as much.

• • •

What are the seventy chores a woman must do?

Cooking and 69.

• • •

TOP TEN REASONS WHY A DOG IS BETTER THAN A WOMAN

1. A dog does not shop.
2. The later you are, the happier a dog is to see you.
3. A dog never expects flowers on Valentine's Day.
4. A dog does not get mad at you if you pet another dog.
5. A dog does not care about the previous dogs in your life.
6. A dog will not get mad at you if you forget its birthday.
7. A dog never expects you to telephone.
8. A dog limits its time in the bathroom to a quick drink.
9. A dog loves you when you leave your clothes on the floor.
10. A dog's parents will never visit you.

• • •

A streetwalker was visiting her doctor for a regular checkup.

"Any specific problems you should tell me about?" the doctor asked.

"I have noticed lately that if I get even the tiniest cut, it seems to bleed for hours," she replied. "Do you think I might be a hemophiliac?"

"Well," the doctor answered, "hemophilia is a genetic disorder, and it is more often found in men, but it is possible for a woman to be a hemophiliac. Tell me, how much do you lose when you have your period?" the doctor inquired.

After calculating for a moment, the hooker replied, "Oh, about seven or eight hundred dollars, I guess."

• • •

What's the difference between a nine-months pregnant woman and a Playboy *centerfold?*

None, if the pregnant woman's husband knows what's good for him.

• • •

Three third-graders—a Jewish kid, an Italian kid, and a redneck kid—are on the playground at recess.

The Jewish kid suggests that they play a new game. "Lets see who has the largest penis," he says.

"Okay," they all agree. So the Jewish kid pulls down his zipper and whips it out.

"That's nothing," says the Italian kid. He whips his out. His is a couple of inches longer.

Now, not to be outdone, the redneck kid whips his out. It is by far the biggest, dwarfing the other two in both length and girth. The Jewish kid and the Italian kid are stunned and amazed. "Wow, that thing is huge!" they exclaim in unison.

That night, the redneck kid's mother asks him what he did at school today. "Oh, we worked on a science project, had a math test, and read out loud from a new book . . . and during recess my friends and I played 'Let's see who has the largest penis.'"

"What kind of game is that, honey?" asks the mother.

"Well, me, Sidney, and Anthony each pulled out our cranks, and I had the biggest! The other kids say it's because I'm a redneck. Is that true, Mom?

"No, honey. It's because you're twenty-three."

• • •

At work one day, a brunette, a redhead, and a blonde all walk into an elevator together. When they get in, they notice a puddle of white fluid on the floor.

The brunette says, "Boy, that sure looks like cum to me."

The redhead bends down and smells it. "It sure smells like cum," she says.

The blonde leans over, sticks her finger in it, and touches it to her tongue. She says, "Well, it's no one in *this* building!"

• • •

Needing a new hinge for a door at home, an attractive young woman walks into a hardware store.

She finds the hinge she's looking for, and as she takes it to the counter, the clerk asks, "Wanna screw for that hinge?"

She replies, "No, but I'll blow you for that toaster on the top shelf."

• • •

An extremely drunk man, looking for a whorehouse, stumbles into a foot doctor's office instead, and weaves over to the receptionist.

Without looking up, she waves him over to the examination bed and says, "Stick it through that curtain."

Looking forward to something kinky, the drunk pulls out his member and sticks it through the crack in the curtains.

"That's not a foot!" screams the receptionist.

"Shit, lady," the drunk says, "I never knew you had a minimum!"

• • •

Lila Mae asks her husband, Zeke, if he'd like breakfast. "How about bacon and eggs, or a slice of toast with some grape jam?" she says.

"I'm not hungry," Zeke says. "It's the Viagra; it's really taken the edge off my appetite."

At lunchtime, Lila Mae asks, "Would you like a bowl of soup or a ham-and-cheese sandwich?"

"I'm not hungry," Zeke says. "It's the Viagra; it's really taken the edge off my appetite."

At dinnertime, Lila Mae offers to run to the café.

"I could pick you up a burger and fries, or even chicken fingers and nachos," she says.

"No, thanks," Zeke says. "It's the Viagra, it's really taken the edge off my appetite."

"Well, can you please get off of me?" she says. "I'm starving!"

• • •

Why are men like public toilets?

They're always vacant, or engaged, or full of shit.

• • •

Why did God give women legs?

So you wouldn't have to drag them into the bathroom and douche them after fucking them.

• • •

The attractive young thing was about to go to bed with her blind date when she burst into tears.

"I'm afraid you'll get the wrong idea about me," she said between sobs. "I'm really not that kind of girl!"

"I believe ya," her date said as he tried to comfort her.

"You're the first one," she gulped.

"The first one to make love to you?" he asked.

"No!" she replied. "The first one to believe me."

• • •

What do you call sex with a black man?

Rape.

• • •

What was one of the reasons the faggot quarter-back couldn't make it in the NFL?

Every time the linemen bent over, he'd get a hard-on.

• • •

The dean of women at an exclusive girls' school was lecturing her students on sexual morality. "We live today in very difficult times for young people. In moments of temptation," she said, "ask yourself just one question: Is an hour of pleasure worth a lifetime of shame?"

A young woman rose in the back of the room and said, "Excuse me, but how do you make it last an hour?"

• • •

There is an eighty-year-old virgin who suddenly gets an itch in her crotch. She goes to the doctor, who checks her out and tells her she has crabs. She explains that she couldn't have crabs because she's a virgin, but the doctor doesn't believe her, so she goes to get a second opinion.

The second doctor gives her the same answer. So she goes to a third doctor and says, "Please help me. This itch is killing me, and I know that I don't have crabs, because I'm a virgin."

The doctor checks her out and says, "I have good news and bad news. The good news is you don't have crabs; the bad news is that your cherry rotted and you have fruit flies."

• • •

A carpet layer had just finished installing carpet for a lady. He stepped out for a smoke, only to realize that he had lost his cigarettes. When he reentered the house, he noticed a bump under the carpet, in the middle of the room.

"No sense pulling up the entire floor for one pack of smokes," he said to himself. He proceeded to take his hammer and flatten the bump.

As he was cleaning up, the lady came in. "Here," she said, handing him his pack of cigarettes. "I found them in the hallway. Now," she said, "if only I could find my daughter's pet hamster."

• • •

After discovering her young daughter playing doctor with the neighbor's boy, the angry mother grabbed the boy by the ear and dragged him to his house and confronted his mother.

"It's only natural for young boys and girls to explore their sexuality by playing doctor at their age," the neighbor said.

"Sexuality, my ass!" the mother yelled. "He took out her appendix!"

• • •

A man walks up to a woman in his office and tells her that her hair smells nice. The woman immediately goes into her supervisor's office and tells him that she wants to file a sexual harassment suit, explaining why.

The supervisor is puzzled by this and says, "What's wrong with a coworker telling you your hair smells nice?"

The woman replies, "He's a midget."

• • •

Three girls are sitting in the doctor's office: a blonde, a redhead, and a brunette. They are all pregnant.

The redhead says, "I'm going to have a boy because I was on the bottom."

The brunette says, "I'm going to have a girl because I was on top."

The blonde starts crying, and the others say, "What's the matter?"

The blonde says, "I'm gonna have puppies!"

• • •

Morris, an elderly gentleman, came home one night to find a homeless girl of about seventeen ransacking his home. He grabbed her by the arm and was just about to call the police when the girl dropped down on her knees and pleaded, "Please don't call the police, mister, oh, please! If you don't, I'll let you make love to me and do whatever you want with my body!"

Morris thought for a moment and decided to give in.

Soon they were naked in bed together.

The old man tried hard to get aroused, but finally, after about fifteen minutes, he rolled over, exhausted and embarrassed.

"I'm sorry, young lady, but it's no use," he gasped. "I'm afraid I'm going to have to call the police after all."

• • •

What has over ten million legs and still can't walk?

Jerry's Kids.

• • •

What has two legs and bleeds?

Half a dog.

• • •

What's gross?

Giving someone a titty twister.

What's grosser than that?

Keeping the nipple.

• • •

What's the definition of gross?

When you open your refrigerator and your rump roast farts at you.

• • •

Then there was the fellow who dreamed that he was eating chocolate ice cream.

When he woke up, he had a spoon in his ass!

• • •

What goes, "ha ha ha ha ha ha ha klunk"?

A leper laughing his ass off.

• • •

What's worse than the pimples on Jeffrey Dahmer's face?

The blackheads in his refrigerator.

• • •

What's twelve inches long and stiff in the morning?

A sudden infant death syndrome victim.

• • •

How do you know a blonde has just lost her virginity?

Her crayons are still sticky.

• • •

What's brown and smells nice?

A big turd in a bubble bath.

• • •

What's twenty feet long and smells like piss?

The conga line at an old-age home.

• • •

What's the definition of African-American aristocracy?

A man who can trace his lineage back to his father.

• • •

"Mommy, Mommy! Why is daddy running away?"

"Shut up, and help me reload the shotgun!"

• • •

"Mommy, Mommy! I don't like fishing."

"Shut up and stop squirming!"

• • •